MW00582472

deeplove

Drs. Les & Leslie Parrott

OUTREACH®

Deep Love
© 2016 by Outreach, Inc.

Published by Outreach, Inc., Colorado Springs, CO 80919

www.Outreach.com

ISBN: 9781635100433

Cover Design by Tim Downs
Interior Design by Alexia Garaventa

Printed in the United States of America

TRANSFORM YOUR RELATIONSHIP WITH THE DEEP LOVE ASSESSMENT

Deep Love is a unique and powerful online assessment that takes just 15 minutes to complete. It generates a personalized 10-page report for couples (whether dating, engaged, or married for decades). Your personalized Deep Love Report can be explored in small groups, classes, or simply on your own as a couple. Each of the four sections of the report—Personality, Communication, Conflict, and Adaptability—are essential to deepening your relationship with lasting, positive results.

OUTREACH.DEEPLOVEASSESSMENT.COM

LEARN MORE AND PURCHASE THE DEEP LOVE ASSESSMENT FOR JUST $35 PER COUPLE!

CONTENTS

INTRODUCTION

---

*If I speak in the tongues of men or of angels,
but do not have love, I am only a resounding
gong or a clanging cymbal.*

1 Corinthians 13:1

"What is the *summum bonum*—the supreme good?"

With this question, professor Henry Drummond began his famous lecture "The Greatest Thing in the World." The year was 1883 as he stood before a classroom of college students and drove home the question: "You have life before you. Once only you can live it. What is the noblest object of desire, the supreme gift to covet?"

The rhetorical question required no reply. Everyone knew the answer. Love. Love is the ultimate good. It lifts us outside ourselves. Love sees beyond the normal range of human vision—over walls of resentment and barriers of betrayal. Love rises above the petty demands and conflicts of life and inspires our spirits to transcend what we are tempted to settle for: decent but merely mediocre. Love aims higher. Unencumbered by self-absorption, love charms us to reach our ideal. Love allures us with a hint of what might be possible. No question about it. Love is the *summum bonum*—"the most excellent way."

And no words, no passage, no song or poem in all of human history has crystallized the qualities of love into simple absolutes more elegantly than 1 Corinthians 13. The Love Chapter of the Bible paints a perfect picture of love. It reveals the kind of ideal love everyone yearns for. But something about these words, the way they are written, tells us they are not meant to be only admired but also lived. These words are a means to a more excellent way of being.

While the passage draws a profile of ideal love, it is too plain for a mere mystic. Paul, the writer of these words, was surely inspired beyond description. He was lifted outside himself as he penned these words. But the passage is not a fantasy of what might be nice. It is a serious essay on how love can be lived. Love is patient. It is not jealous, does not get angry quickly. These are qualities ordinary people can cultivate to build extraordinary relationships.

The challenge, of course, is to find ways of bringing these heavenly qualities into our earthly reality. The challenge is to plunge beneath the surface and sink the roots of our relationships firmly in love.

That's exactly why we designed the Deep Love Assessment. If you're not already familiar with it, the Deep Love Assessment is a self-guided experience that begins when a couple answers a series of questions, independently, to generate a personalized, ten-page report on their relationship (see Outreach.DeepLoveAssessment.com). Don't worry. It's not something you pass or fail. It's a fun and proven way to experience a deeper connection.

And this little book of sixteen meditations coordinates beautifully with each page of your Deep Love Report. We recommend reading these meditations in tandem with your Deep Love Report.

With every good wish and prayer,

Drs. Les & Leslie Parrott
Seattle, Washington

PERSONALITY

Love is the only way
to grasp another human being
in the innermost core
of his personality.

Viktor Frankl

YOUR RELATIONSHIP IS ONE OF A KIND

A long marriage is two people
trying to dance a duet and two solos
at the same time.

Anne Taylor Fleming

Some call it your temperament. Some call it your nature or your character. Mystics call it your spirit. Whatever you call it, we all have one, and like a fingerprint, each one is totally and completely one of a kind. In spite of all the similarities we share as human beings, that tiny .01 percent difference in our genes makes each of us unique. How? Because we inherit three billion pairs of nucleotides, or chemical bases of genetic information, from our moms and our dads. So even a .01 percent difference is still three million chemical distinctions. And that's a lot!

It's tough to comprehend. Think of it this way: There are more than three million differences between your genome and anyone else's. And it's these three million different sources of genetic information that make your personality exceptional.

Of course, the same holds true for your spouse. Your marriage brings together two completely unique and special personalities. There has never been a combination like you two before. In all of human history, marriage has never witnessed your inimitable combination of personalities. Your relationship is unprecedented. It is unmatched.

> And even the very hairs of your head are all numbered.
>
> *Matthew 10:30*

That's why you may have found that what seems to work wonders for another couple doesn't help the two of you much at all. We have some friends who married about the same time we did, almost twenty-five years ago. If you ask them what keeps their marriage strong, they'll tell you that they have learned never to fight.

"We have frank discussions, but we never raise our voices," one of them will say. "We've learned to discipline ourselves, and we always count to ten when that starts to happen."

"You've got to be kidding!" Les counters. "Is that humanly possible in married life?"

"It works for us," they say with a smile.

And it does. They're a very happy couple. But we will be the first to tell you that doesn't jibe with our own married life. Not that we have frequent yelling matches. Not at all. Gratefully, we've learned to curb much of our conflict over the years, but it's had little to do with counting to ten.

The point is that every couple is unique. It's what caused German poet Heinrich Heine to liken marriage to "the high sea for which no compass has yet been invented." So what would you two say makes you the most unique as a couple? In other words, when you consider how God hardwired your personalities and how the two of you come together, what makes your relationship matchless?

ENJOYING OUR DIFFERENCES

*We continue to shape
our personality all our life.*

Albert Camus

It has been suggested that two strangers off the street could be married to each other and make a pretty good marriage if only they were mature enough to work their way through the inevitable differences.

How do you and your partner handle differences? If you are like most couples, you probably try one of two things: either you sweep your differences under the rug by ignoring them altogether, or you try to make your partner become like yourself. Unfortunately, both strategies are doomed to frustration. For one thing, it is only a matter of time before repressed differences reemerge, and second, we miss out on a tremendous gift of marriage when we do not enjoy our partner's uniqueness. That's right, *enjoy* the differences!

Every person is unique (see Psalm 139:14). God never intended couples to approach life as if they were twins separated at birth. He made us with unique strengths and weaknesses. He gave each of us special gifts.

The differences in temperament that allow your partner to deal with situations that would drive you crazy are something to be thankful for. Sure, some of your partner's traits make living together tough at times, but appreciating the positive side of your differences will make your marriage more balanced and complete.

And don't undervalue the predictability that comes in our personalities. "I knew you were going to say that." How many times have you and your spouse uttered these words to one another? If you're like most couples, married for even a short while, you've come to expect certain reactions and behaviors from your spouse. Why? Because personalities are fundamentally predictable. Thank God!

Can you imagine trying to be married if you never knew what to expect from your spouse? A marriage couldn't survive if behavior was not basically predictable. Imagine if one day your spouse was extremely laid-back and easygoing and then the next day was extremely intense and regimented. You'd be living in chaos. Without relative consistency from your spouse, marriage would be an unbearable roller-coaster ride.

Now, we've all had married moments when we've said something like: "I would never have predicted *you* would want to do that!" Even with a relatively consistent set of traits, our personalities make room for a smidgen of the unpredictable. And that's not bad. Changing things up on occasion can get us out of boring ruts. But for the most part, you can take comfort in knowing that your spouse's personality (as well as your own) will remain pretty predictable.

Take a moment right now to note a character quality in your spouse's personality that gives you comfort, a trait that you are especially thankful for today, and explain why.

> Make me truly happy by agreeing wholeheartedly with each other, loving one another, and working together with one mind and purpose.
>
> *Philippians 2:2 (NLT)*

COMMUNICATION

*Good communication
is as stimulating as black coffee.*

Anne Morrow Lindbergh

I'M TALKING HERE

---

*My wife says I never listen to her
. . . at least I think that's what she says.*

Anonymous

Old Fred's hospital bed is surrounded by well-wishers, but it doesn't look good. Suddenly, he motions frantically to the pastor for something to write on. The pastor lovingly hands him a pen and a piece of paper. Fred uses his last bit of energy to scribble a note and then dies.

The pastor thinks it best not to look at the note right away, so he places it in his jacket pocket. At Fred's funeral, as the pastor is finishing his eulogy, he realizes he's wearing the jacket he was wearing when Fred died.

"Fred handed me a note just before he died," he says. "I haven't looked at it, but knowing Fred, I'm sure there's a word of inspiration in it for us all."

Opening the note, he reads aloud, "Help! You're standing on my oxygen hose!"

Ever felt as utterly ignored as Fred did when trying to communicate? Ever felt like your urgent message just wasn't getting through? It's not uncommon in most marriages. Even when we feel like what we have to say is critically important, our spouse can squash it without even knowing.

> *She:* Oh, I've been wanting to tell you what happened with Jody today at the office.
>
> *He:* Hey, that reminds me—tomorrow before I go to work, I need you to pick up some dry cleaning for me if you can.
>
> *She:* Okay. So Jody got some information about how I'm going to—
>
> *He (interrupting):* So you'll pick it up for me in time for work?
>
> *She (frustrated):* I said yes!
>
> *He:* Good. So what's Jody doing?
>
> *She:* Oh, never mind.

Of course, she's still dying to tell her mate about Jody, but she's testing to see if he really wants to hear about it or not.

> *He:* No, c'mon. What's happening with Jody?
>
> *She:* Okay, but I don't want to be interrupted again.

And who can blame her? Nobody likes to get stepped on as they're starting to talk. But it happens. In fact, if you're married to a hard-driving, task-oriented person (what we call an aggressive problem solver), you know this all too well.

The key, of course, is to salvage the conversation before it loses life. It's only natural to test your partner's true motives (do they want to hear me or not?), but you don't want to push too hard. Consider how just one more step would have sent this conversation over the edge.

> *He:* No, c'mon. What's happening with Jody?
>
> *She:* I don't feel like talking about it anymore.
>
> *He:* Okay. I'd like to hear it, but if you want to be that way, then fine.
>
> *She:* Then fine.

Now they're stuck in a rut. They're not going anywhere until one of them surrenders the power struggle. See how easy it is to stifle a perfectly good conversation before it even gets going? Don't allow this to happen to you if you can help it. Give your interruptive spouse the benefit of the doubt. But if you do get to this kind of stalemate, for goodness' sake, don't let it last for long. Take your foot off your partner's proverbial oxygen hose by saying something like: "I'm sorry. I guess I got my feelings hurt when you interrupted me. I know your task was important to you and that you could actually listen better once you got it off your to-do list. I really would like to talk." That's all. A simple apology and invitation are all it takes to breathe new life back into a conversation that's on life support.

> My dear brothers and sisters, take note of this: Everyone should be quick to listen, slow to speak.
>
> *James 1:19*

DO YOU HEAR WHAT I'M NOT SAYING?

When we talk to family members, we search for signs of love but become attuned to signs of disapproval.

Deborah Tannen

Your message is determined more by *how* you say it than by *what* you actually say. Consider a seemingly simple sentence and how the emphasis on different words can change the message:

> With pleasure: You're wearing that sweater.
>
> With disgust: You're wearing THAT sweater.
>
> With surprise: YOU'RE wearing that sweater?

Your partner hears what isn't being said with mere words alone. And it speaks volumes. How you say something (and the context in which it is said) is more important than the actual words you use to say it.

Let's make this clear. What we say to each other is only a small part of the communication process. How we say it—with a smile, a shrug, a frown, or a glare—conveys so much more. Some communication experts say that as much as 90 percent of our communication is not conveyed by the actual words we use. Whether you like it or not, you are saying a great deal more with your tone and your body than you are with your words.

Consider eye contact. Whether or not you are maintaining eye contact reveals how genuinely interested you are in understanding your spouse. But not only do good conversationalists do a lot of eye-to-eye gazing, scientists have found that your pupils actually dilate, an involuntary response indicating pleasure at what you see. Amazing, isn't it? Your eyes really are windows to your soul. By the way, you can't fake the size of your pupil dilation. Either you're genuinely interested or you're not. Your eyes won't lie.

Eye contact isn't the only nonverbal clue to a couple's relationship. Unhappy couples, according to researcher John Gottman, exhibit a wide array of gestures and body language that gives away their estrangement. They lean away from each other; there's more rigidness and lots of rolling of eyes and crossing of arms. Gottman's research shows that women who are unhappy often unconsciously roll back their upper lip while they talk. And both men and women who are contemptuous of their spouse will tilt their head back and literally look down their nose at their spouse, as if sniffing something unpleasant.

Loving couples, on the other hand, often touch each other while they talk, and that doesn't necessarily mean something as conventional as holding hands. A pat on the forearm, brushing a stray thread off a lapel, or even intertwining feet are tender ways of intensifying the verbal connection. These couples also lean close to each other, as if a magnet were at work.

> Set a guard over my mouth, Lord; keep watch over the door of my lips.
>
> *Psalm 141:3*

The bottom line on nonverbal communication? If you are relying on words alone to communicate to each other, you are fooling yourselves. Research has found that husbands and wives are quite accurate interpreters of their spouses' nonverbal communication. In fact, husbands whose wives send clear messages through facial expressions reported fewer complaints in their marriage. Nonverbal communication is critically important to helping you understand and be understood.

INTIMACY

Adam and his wife were both naked,
and they felt no shame.

Genesis 2:25

LIVEN UP YOUR LOVE TALK

A bore is a fellow talking who can change the subject back to his topic of conversation faster than you can change it back to yours.

Laurence J. Peter

Ever felt like your talking was putting someone, namely your partner, to sleep? If so, you may be in the same company as Supreme Court Justice Michael Eakin, who decided to spice up what he had to say in his courtroom by dispensing poetic justice and delivering his rulings in rhyming couplets. For real. One example is in the Pennsylvania Supreme Court case involving a woman who claimed that a lie about an engagement ring should void a prenuptial agreement.

Eakin wrote, "A groom must expect matrimonial pandemonium / when his spouse finds he's given her a cubic zirconium / instead of a diamond in her engagement band / the one he said was worth twenty-one grand."

"You have an obligation as a judge to be right," Eakin later told a reporter, "but you have no obligation to be dull."

Well, that's one way to make what you have to say more interesting. But unless you have a poetic inspiration to express your love in verse, we don't recommend talking in rhyme to your partner. On the other hand, we do recommend steering clear of tedious talk. Of course, what's tedious to one person is fascinating to another.

> *He:* If I upgrade the memory on this old computer, we can use it for the kids' educational software and they won't have to use mine.
>
> *She:* Okay.
>
> *He:* I'm thinking another couple megs of RAM would do the trick.
>
> *She:* Uh-huh.
>
> *He:* Of course, if I install a wireless hub—well, no, I don't think I want to do that.
>
> *She: (Yawn)*

He: They're coming out with a new model in a few months, and that's the time to look into that. Right?

She: I guess.

Are you asleep yet? You can bet this man's wife is ready to doze off—and he doesn't even know it. That's the point. Boredom strikes a conversation when one person has no idea how boring he's become. After all, he's enthralled with computers. He subscribes to computer magazines. He loves visiting computer stores. His wife, on the other hand, finds computer talk about as exciting as airline food.

> A word fitly spoken is like apples of gold in a setting of silver.
>
> *Proverbs 25:11 (ESV)*

What should this couple do? By all means, talk about it—tactfully. She needs to let him know she's happy that he enjoys his computer hobby. But she also needs to let him know this subject is dull and tedious to her. She owes it to him. And he owes it to her, eventually, to shift gears to a more mutually satisfying topic of conversation.

This doesn't mean he should never bring up computers again, not at all. In fact, it may mean she needs to exert a bit more effort in finding something she can enjoy about his hobby. But it also means he needs to be a bit more sensitive to her natural inclinations and interests when he gets carried away. He needs to clue into the fact that she's bored.

Every couple has dull spots, the places where one partner feels like he or she is sitting through an industrial training film. So wise up. Pay attention to those topics and how you're coming off to your partner. If you can laugh at yourself when you get carried away with something that's putting your partner to sleep, all the better. In fact, this may even be the time to follow Judge Eakin's example and speak in rhyme. If you're brave.

WHAT MOVIE TITLE DESCRIBES YOUR SEX LIFE?

The instinct of fidelity is perhaps the deepest instinct in the great complex we call sex. Where there is real sex there is the underlying passion for fidelity.

D. H. Lawrence

We were speaking at a large marriage conference not long ago, and after one of our sessions, we slid into a workshop by Pam and Rich Batten, whose title caught our eye: "How to Have Kids and a Sex Life, Too." They warmed up the group by asking couples which movie title best described their sex life: *The Fast and the Furious*, *What's the Worst That Could Happen?* or *The Mummy*

Returns. There wasn't a show of hands, but *Dr. Dolittle* got the most chuckles.

In the discussion that followed, couples were quick to rattle off obstacles to a satisfactory love life: no energy, no privacy, no spontaneity, kids banging on doors, kids barging in, and so on. Each complaint engendered nods and groans of agreement. It seems nearly every couple, married long enough, understands the struggle to keep their sex life filled with passion. What most couples don't understand is how an intentional effort—once every thirty days—can keep the flames of passion burning.

Let's make this clear. Sex is critically important for a quality marriage. We'll say it again. Sex makes a significant impact on whether or not you will rate your marriage as satisfying.

In one survey on the importance of sex for marriage, the results were compelling: Couples who rated their sex lives positively also rated their marriages positively, and those who rated their sex lives negatively rated their marriages negatively as well. In other words, if couples report that sex is unimportant to them, it is very likely that they view their entire marriage as unhappy. Both the quantity and quality of sex in marriage are central to an overall good relationship.

You might be relieved to know that a number of factors other than frequency of sexual interaction have also been linked to satisfaction with marital sex. Mutuality in initiating sex can be an important contributor to sexual satisfaction for both wives and husbands. It also appears that women who take an active role during sex are more likely to be pleased with their sex lives than those who assume a more passive role.

No study states that a high-quality sex life is an absolute requirement for a high-quality marriage or that a good sex life guarantees a good marriage. Nonetheless, studies consistently suggest that quality of sex and quality of marriage do go together in most cases. That's why this topic is so important for married couples to discuss. So how's your sex life?

That's a fair question, isn't it? After all, sexuality is not a given, something that somehow miraculously takes care of itself once we enter marriage. It needs nurture, tenderness, education, and—are you ready for this?—religion.

It's a fact. Religion, according to some studies, is good for your sex life. As strange as it may sound, there is a strong link in marriage between spirituality and sexuality. Married couples who cultivate spiritual intimacy are far more likely to report higher satisfaction with their sex life than other couples.

This fact makes sense if you think about it. The mysteries, wonders, and pleasures of sex in marriage are a divine gift to celebrate. Those who try to limit sex to procreation are simply ignoring the Bible. Scripture—right from the beginning—enthusiastically affirms sex within the bonds of marriage. In the Old Testament and in the New Testament, in the Gospels and in the Epistles, we find the call to celebrate sexuality in marriage. There is no denying that your spiritual growth helps to enhance your sexual intimacy in marriage. So, we'll ask it again. How's your sex life?

> Since they are no longer two but one, let no one split apart what God has joined together.
>
> *Matthew 19:6 (NLT)*

CONFLICT

No pressure, no diamonds.

Mary Case

DON'T TALK WHILE I'M INTERRUPTING YOU

*A good listener is a good talker
with a sore throat.*

Katharine Whitehorn

Professional golfer Tommy Bolt was playing in Los Angeles and had a caddy with a reputation of constant chatter. Before they teed off, Bolt told him, "Don't say a word to me. And if I ask you something, just answer yes or no."

During the round, Bolt found the ball next to a tree, where he had to hit under a branch, over a lake, and onto the green. He got down on his knees, looked through the trees, and sized up the shot.

"What do you think?" he asked the caddy. "Five-iron?"

"No, Mr. Bolt," the caddy said.

"What do you mean, not a five-iron?" Bolt snorted. "Watch this shot."

The caddy rolled his eyes. "No-o-o."

But Bolt hit it, and the ball stopped about two feet from the hole. He turned to his caddy, handed him the five-iron, and said, "Now what do you think about that? You can talk now."

"Mr. Bolt," the caddy said, "that wasn't your ball."

Ouch! That had to hurt.

Ever put the kibosh on your mate's messages? Ever asked him or her to stop talking so much? Perhaps you're thinking that you'd never be so rude. Okay, so let's say you haven't asked directly, but have you ever given every nonverbal signal you could think of to get your spouse to clam up? Be honest. Haven't you had occasions when you simply didn't want to listen? It's this desire that drove Margaret Millar to say, "Most conversations are simply monologues delivered in the presence of a witness."

It's not uncommon or even unkind to want a little peace and quiet while you're concentrating. Trust us, we know of what we speak. In fact, on countless occasions while writing this little book together, one of us would walk into the midst of the other's writing time and begin a conversation. "Shhhh, I'm writing!" was the most common response. A momentary interruption or diversion can throw off all of one's concentration—whether it be while playing golf, writing, or doing anything else.

Each and every one of us sometimes needs our partner not to talk. That's why we have an entire chapter devoted to not talking in our book *Love Talk*.

> The tongue of the wise adorns knowledge, but the mouth of the fool gushes folly.
>
> *Proverbs 15:2*

In fact, it may be one of the only communication books in history that tells you when not to talk. Sounds strange, we know. Not many communication experts devote a lot of time to clamming up. But we are convinced that couples who enjoy the deepest levels of communication have also honed their ability to cultivate a well-timed silence. They know, for example, not to talk when their partner isn't ready to talk. They know not to talk when they are having the same conversation they've had a million times and it's sure to go nowhere again. They know not to talk when they need time to think. And they know not to talk when their partner needs to vent.

"There is nothing so annoying," said Mark Twain, "as to have two people talking when you're busy interrupting." It's true. Sometimes we just need to get it all out, to emote, to talk. We counselors call it "catharsis," a term that literally means to purge or cleanse. And it may be just what the doctor ordered.

So if your partner is fully focused on a specific task or if he or she simply needs to monologue rather than dialogue for a while, try to clam up. Zip your lips. Chances are, the favor will be returned to you someday, and you won't want your spouse to talk while you're busy interrupting.

TICKED OFF

---

*Anger is a wind which blows out
the lamp of the mind.*

Robert Green Ingersoll

O n a trip to London we visited the war rooms
where Winston Churchill worked safely un-
derground during World War II. While there, we
learned that the bombs dropped during this war
are still killing people in Europe. They turn up—and
sometimes blow up—at construction sites, in fish-
ing nets, or on beaches more than fifty years after the guns have fallen silent. Undetected bombs
become more dangerous with time because corro-
sion can expose the detonator.

What is true of bombs that are not dealt with
is also true of unresolved anger. Buried anger ex-
plodes when we least expect it—especially in marriage. Ever felt like you stepped on a buried bomb?
It's not uncommon for most couples. And think of

all the time we waste on anger. After all, it does little for us most of the time. In fact, anger can become quite contagious and cause couples to be irrational.

Consider the story Billy Martin, former New York Yankees manager, told about hunting in Texas with baseball star Mickey Mantle at his friend's ranch. When they reached the ranch, Mantle told Martin to wait in the car while he checked with his friend. Mantle's friend quickly gave them permission to hunt, but he asked Mantle a favor. He had a pet mule that was going blind, and he didn't have the heart to put him out of his misery. He asked Mantle to shoot the mule for him. When Mantle came back to the car, he pretended to be angry. He scowled and slammed the door. Martin asked him what was wrong, and Mantle said his friend wouldn't let them hunt. "I'm so mad at that guy," Mantle said, "I'm going out to his barn to shoot one of his mules!" Mantle drove like a maniac to the barn. Martin protested, but Mantle was adamant. "Just watch me!" he shouted.

When they got to the barn, Mantle jumped out of the car with his rifle, ran inside, and shot the mule. As he was leaving, though, he heard two shots, and he ran back to the car. He saw that Martin had taken out his rifle too. "What are you doing, Martin?" he yelled.

Martin yelled back, face red with anger, "We'll show that son of a gun! I just killed two of his cows!"

Like we said, anger can become dangerously contagious. When you get angry, the probability of your spouse getting angry increases significantly, and vice versa. So what's our point? That anger is almost always a huge time waster in marriage. Does it ever have its place in marriage? That's not an easy answer. Anger is a human emotion and nearly inevitable. So, on the one hand, yes, it has its place. But on the other hand, anger is so rarely used rightly that we're tempted to say no. Here's how Aristotle put it: "Anybody can become angry—that is easy; but to be angry with the right person, and to the right degree, and at the right time, and for the right purpose, and in the right way—that is not within everybody's power and is not easy."

> A quick-tempered person does foolish things.
>
> Proverbs 14:17

The key to being angry the "right way" is to ensure that you are not using your anger to inflict pain or "repay anyone evil for evil," as Paul said in Romans 12:17. In other words, make sure you are not seeking revenge, but leave that up to God.

When you allow this principle to keep your anger in check, you are far more likely to reclaim countless moments in your marriage that would otherwise be given over to the ravages of rage and resentment. Consider the last time you, personally, were angry with your partner. Did you inflict pain on your partner with your anger? If so, how might you better handle an angry situation like that in the future?

FINANCES

Wealth consists not in having great possessions, but in having few wants.

Epictetus

MONEY TALKS AND SO CAN WE

No matter how similar or different
your financial perspectives are, talking to your
spouse about money is rarely easy.

Ron Blue

When it comes to money, Mike is a hoarder. Impoverished as a child and abandoned at nine by parents working as itinerant fruit pickers, he remembers squirreling away spare change and tools. As an adult, he hates to spend money and is happiest when he deposits a check in the bank. "I feel warm and fuzzy inside if I can leave the money sitting there and not touch it," he says. "It's a security thing."

His wife, Janice, on the other hand, is a spender. She grew up in "a stable, little-above-average family" and was provided with all the necessities by a generous father who, nevertheless, tightly controlled the household purse. She likes a bargain but has "no problem spending money. I like to have fun, enjoy life," Janice says.

For eighteen years of marriage, the fiscally different couple found themselves locked in a mostly silent battle over finances. When Janice bought several pairs of Italian leather shoes at a bargain $19.99 each, she hid them behind a chest freezer, bringing out a pair every few months. "Mike would say, 'Are those shoes new?' I'd say, 'Oh, I've had them for a while,'" she recalls. "I would avoid confrontation, lie, sneak around."

Meanwhile, Mike lived in fear of his wife's spending without his knowledge. "I would feel anguish and anger, even over a new pair of shoes," he says. "I was closed; I wouldn't say very much. But I would just be in turmoil about it."

Four years ago, however, their stalemate ended when the couple started going to counseling. That's where they began to talk about money, explore the roots of their attitudes about it, draw up a budget, and even fight about their finances.

Money and marriage. It can be a combustible combination—especially when couples don't talk about it. Whether it be talking about getting out of debt, spending and giving, saving and investing, or planning for retirement, the topic of money can be a tinderbox on the brink of explosion for most couples.

So what's a couple to do? Most experts agree that couples need to schedule a routine time to discuss their money matters. It might be at the end of each month, for example. They need to sit down with their checkbooks and their credit card statements and take stock. "What are we—as a team—doing with our money this month?" is the big question.

Now we can almost hear some of you saying, "Oh, we don't have to talk about money because one of us handles all that." Okay, so one of you is the money manager who pays the bills and balances the books. Good. But you still need to have a time to talk, if only briefly, about your finances.

Leslie describes herself as a "money monk." She doesn't like to admit that it exists. In fact, she doesn't even carry an actual wallet in her purse. Of course, this can drive me [Les] batty. I'm much more money focused than Leslie. So in our relationship, I handle most of the money matters. But that doesn't get Leslie off the hook. We still have a monthly meeting where we review where our money went and what we might like to do differently in the next thirty-day cycle. It's a point of connection that ensures we are on the same page. This discussion is certainly not the conversational highlight of our month, but it has become a conversation we are both comfortable with and it has solved many financial problems before they even occurred.

So how about you? Are you talking about your money together—or just arguing about it? You don't need to have fiscal feuds. Whether you are spenders, savers, or a combination of both, you can't afford to skip this topic of conversation. So right now, set aside a time when you can both come to the table with information and questions about your finances. Get your spending habits and credit card balances out in the open. Hiding from them and each other soon jeopardizes communication in other areas of your relationship. Try to understand the historical basis for you and your partner's attitudes, fears, and anxieties about

> Keep your lives free from the love of money and be content with what you have, because God has said, "Never will I leave you; never will I forsake you."
>
> *Hebrews 13:5*

money. Leave defensiveness and name-calling out of this arena. This is simply a time to talk about where you are with your money and where you'd like to be.

SHOW ME
THE MONEY

Time is the coin of your life. It is the only coin you have, and only you can determine how it will be spent. Be careful lest you let other people spend it for you.

Carl Sandburg

How much money would you need to improve your life? Go ahead, think about this. Talk it over with your spouse. After all, nearly everyone, no matter how much money they have, would like more—believing that it would ease their angst or improve their happiness. So what about you? How much would it take to really make a difference in your life?

Got a figure in mind? Let's see how you stack up with other people.

When asked how much money it would take to make a real difference in their lives, 33 percent of people say that an extra $100,000 in the bank would improve their lot, and 14 percent would want up to $500,000. An even million would shake things up, say 16 percent, and 24 percent calculate it would take up to $10 million.

We're all over the map when it comes to feeling financially fit, which makes sense because money, like time, is relative. The more we have of either one determines how we spend it. And one of the supreme lessons in life seems to be that the less time you have on this earth, the more likely you are to give your money away.

There's a new breed of givers these days known as "engaged philanthropists." Kenneth Behring is a good example. He seemed to have everything. He was affluent and generous. But something transformed him during a trip to Vietnam in 2000. The retired construction magnate was helping a relief organization bring food and medicine to a village. It was there that Behring personally delivered a wheelchair to a six-year-old polio victim. The girl's reaction changed his life—so much so that he created the Wheelchair Foundation, which today delivers ten thousand wheelchairs a month worldwide.

You don't have to be a wealthy benefactor in order to adopt a hands-on approach to giving. In fact, it doesn't matter how much money you have, giving is good for your marriage.

We know that agreeing on financial matters in marriage is not always easy. It can be an emotional proposition. We certainly don't always see eye to eye on finances in our home. But a fundamental shift of attitude toward giving took place when we changed the question we were asking of each other. Rather than asking, "How much of our money should we give to God?" we learned to ask, "How much of God's money should we spend on ourselves?" The difference between these two questions was monumental for us. With this understanding—that our income is all God's—as a starting point, we eliminated much of the legalistic thinking and guilt related to giving based on a set percentage of income. John Wesley understood this when he said, "Gain all you can, save all you can, give all you can."

> Be generous: Invest in acts of charity. Charity yields high returns.
>
> *Ecclesiastes 11:1 (MSG)*

Only 13 percent of the population believes money can buy happiness. But almost everyone believes that giving generously to others brings great joy. And it does. So consider how the two of you might spend some time doing a little hands-on helping. It may be one of the most important investments you ever make in your marriage.

ADAPTABILITY

*To the man who only has a hammer,
everything he encounters begins to
look like a nail.*

Abraham H. Maslow

HOUSTON, WE HAVE AN ATTITUDE PROBLEM

The problem is not that there are problems.
The problem is expecting otherwise and thinking
that having problems is a problem.

Theodore Rubin

In April 1970, the spacecraft *Apollo 13* was crippled by an in-flight explosion. The astronauts relied on archaic navigational techniques to get back home. A slight miscalculation could have sent the ship spiraling thousands of miles off course into outer space. Even if navigation back into Earth's orbit succeeded, fears remained that the heat shield and parachutes were not functional. In addition, a tropical storm was brewing in the landing zone.

As a press agent recounted the multitude of dangers facing the crew, the NASA official who he was interviewing, clearly stressed, responded, "I know what the problems are, Henry. It will be the worst disaster NASA's ever experienced."

A NASA chief overheard this pessimistic assessment and responded sharply, "With all due respect, I believe this is going to be our finest hour."

A mixture of fear and hope etched the faces of the NASA team, as well as the friends and family of the astronauts, as they watched for any sign of a successful reentry. Three minutes after the reentry process began, Walter Cronkite's voice informed the viewing audience that no space capsule had taken longer than three minutes to complete reentry. A NASA employee continued to attempt to contact the Command Module *Odyssey*, saying, "*Odyssey*, this is Houston. Do you read me?" The silence was agonizing. Suddenly, the receiver at NASA crackled. A capsule seemed to materialize out of thin air on the screen, and the parachutes looked like giant flowers that had burst into bloom.

A voice responded loud and clear, "Hello, Houston. This is *Odyssey*. It's good to see you again."

Few of us will ever be called upon to solve such a nail-biting and complex problem as this, but that doesn't mean our problem-solving strategies are necessarily any different from NASA's. Notice how one official in this true story looked at the problem pessimistically, emphasizing the potential disaster, while another official viewed the problem as an opportunity—one that would live on in the history books as their finest hour. Does this attitudinal difference actually impact problem-solving? You bet.

> A cheerful heart is good medicine, but a crushed spirit dries up the bones.
>
> *Proverbs 17:22*

Research on problem-solving approaches in marriage shows us that an upbeat attitude goes a long way in helping couples survive and thrive in trying times. "Creativity in finding potential solutions," says researcher Martin Seligman, "is far more likely among those with an optimistic perspective." Makes sense. Optimists are not only more creative but also more persistent. They keep at a problem until it is conquered—especially in marriage.

A pessimistic partner seems to get stuck on pointing out what's wrong. It may not be their intention, but they curdle action, imagination, and initiative. Of course, we all have bouts of pessimism, but some of us linger in it a little too long. The telltale symptom? If you are stuck in the rut of a problem (keeping the house clean, paying bills on time, disciplining the kids consistently), you may be marinating in the malaise of a negative perspective. And it's time for an attitude checkup.

In fact, the problem with your problem may be your attitude. It's difficult to exaggerate the power of your perspective on your ability to solve problems together. So take inventory. Fess up. Do you need an attitude realignment? Most of us do at one time or another. So consider this a reminder to do just that. And keep this suggestion from famed poet Maya Angelou in mind: "If you don't like something, change it. If you can't change it, change your attitude. Don't complain."

COPING WITH ATMOSPHERIC CONDITIONS

Most folks are about as happy
as they make their minds up to be.

Abraham Lincoln

We had just finished speaking at a camp in the San Juan Islands when a small plane buzzed overhead and landed on a nearby airstrip. A few minutes later the pilot was flying us over the islands of Puget Sound, and we were approaching the lights of a local airport. "The most important thing about landing is the attitude of the plane," said the pilot.

"You mean altitude, don't you?" we asked.

"No," the pilot explained. "The attitude has to do with the nose of the plane. If the attitude is too high, the plane will come down with a severe bounce. And if the attitude is too low, the plane may go out of control because of excessive landing speed."

Then the pilot said something that got our attention: *"The trick is to get the right attitude in spite of atmospheric conditions."*

Without knowing it, our pilot had given us a perfect analogy for creating happiness in marriage—developing the right attitude in spite of the circumstances we find ourselves in.

It is no accident that some couples who encounter marital turbulence navigate it successfully while others in similar circumstances are dominated by frustration, disappointment, and eventual despair. It is no accident, also, that some couples are radiant, positive, and happy while other couples are beaten down, defeated, and anxiety ridden.

Researchers who have searched for the difference between the two have come up with all kinds of correlates to marital success (long courtships, similar backgrounds, supportive families, good communication, well educated, and so on). But the bottom line is that happy couples *decide* to be happy. In spite of whatever life deals them, they make happiness a habit. They don't give in or resign themselves to what happens. They *do* something.

This is precisely what researcher Martin Seligman and others found in experiments with both animals and people. When dogs were strapped in a harness and given repeated shocks, with no opportunity to avoid them, they felt helpless—obviously. But later, when placed in another situation where they *could* escape the punishment by merely leaping a hurdle, these same dogs cowered without hope. Faced with traumatic events over which they have no control, people, too, come to feel helpless and hopeless. This was discovered near the end of World War II when death camp prisoners were being released, only to discover they could have easily escaped on their own through holes in fences and unlocked gates. It's what researchers call "learned helplessness." And it's the price we pay for giving up control.

> You must have the same attitude that Christ Jesus had.
>
> *Philippians 2:5 (NLT)*

Whether or not you are in control doesn't seem to be the ultimate issue. It's whether you *believe* you have control that really counts. Think about it. Because we can reduce the intensity of our stress by simply thinking about our problems in a more positive light, we have within us the ability to control the effect that adversity has on us. We have the capacity to find the right attitude in spite of atmospheric conditions.

TIME

*Time is your life—nothing more,
nothing less. The way you spend your
hours and your days is the way you
spend your life.*

John Boykin

LIFE IN THE FAST LANE

Running on empty, running blind.
Running into the sun, but I'm running behind.

Jackson Browne

Dale Rooks, a school crossing guard in Florida, tried everything to get cars to slow down through the school zone where he was in charge. But nothing worked. Not until he took a blow-dryer and wrapped it in electrical tape, making it look like a radar gun.

The next day Dale just pointed the thing at cars, and incredibly, drivers began to slam on their breaks. "It's almost comical," Dale said. "It's amazing how well it works."

Dale's clever idea got us thinking about what it would take to get people to slow down in general—not just in their cars. Imagine if your spouse could hold up a radar gun when you were falling victim to hurry sickness. On a day when you were particularly rushed and busy, your partner could clock your speed and pull you over for a little respite. Wouldn't that be convenient?

We started thinking about what it would be like to pull out a radar gun from a holster when either one of us is rushing through our day, too busy to connect or even pause for a meal. Or how about if we could cite our partner for speeding through their day? What if we could give our spouse a "speeding ticket" when they get too rushed? And maybe after three tickets in an allotted period of time, they would have to go on vacation with us.

It's all wishful thinking, we know. But it does give one pause to consider how we might help each other slow down. Jonathan Tunrbough tells the story of his mother, who was driving his sisters and him to school one day when she was pulled over by a policeman for speeding. After things were worked out with the officer, his mom took off again. She was being very careful to stay under the speed limit. After a few minutes had passed, they all started hearing a strange noise coming from their vehicle. "What's that noise?" his mother asked. Laughing, he replied, "That's the sound of slow. We've never heard it before!"

What does slow sound like in your marriage? Seriously, what does it sound like and look like? Chances are, one of you is currently wanting the other to slow down, or maybe both of you realize you've got to ease up on your pace. Lots of couples will say, "We've just got to slow down." Okay. But what does that look like in tangible terms? In other words, how will you know when you've slowed down?

> Teach us to number our days, that we may gain a heart of wisdom.
>
> *Psalm 90:12*

For us, a sure sign of slowing down means both of us being home with our boys for an evening with nothing scheduled past 5:00 p.m. except time together. It also means not holding phone conferences while driving in the car with the rest of the family present. It means being able to take our little ones to the park without a time limit. And the sound of slowness in our home means hearing casual conversation around the dinner table. It means hearing the waves on the beach in our neighborhood while we're taking in the sunset together.

So we'll ask you again. What are the sounds and sights of slow in your relationship? Answering this question just might help you find more of them.

SLOW DOWN, YOU MOVE TOO FAST

A person is always startled when he hears himself seriously called an old man for the first time.

Oliver Wendell Holmes

What did you have for dinner last night? How about what you wore last Tuesday? Can't recall? You're not alone. Research reveals that our brains click into autopilot when it comes to routine behaviors. And that seems to make time pass faster.

Psychologist Dinah Avni-Babad at the Hebrew University in Jerusalem discovered that routine actions are rarely remembered while new experiences find a solid place in our memory banks. Even though it seems counterintuitive, routine is a form of inaction, she says. "When you tell people routine makes things go faster, they say, 'Hmm. Can't be.'"

As we age, we encounter fewer new experiences so it feels as though time passes more quickly. "The days feel much, much longer when you're a child," Avni-Babad says. Want time to pass more slowly? Shake up your life, suggests the research. Get out of your rut and try something new.

Of course, that's not always as easy as it sounds. Some of us are stuck in a rut because we like it. We don't have to think about much when we follow our routine. But that's the point! Because we're not thinking about it, time slips by more rapidly.

To illustrate how inane we can become when stuck in a rut, we want to point out that the U.S. standard railroad gauge is four feet eight and one-half inches. How did we wind up with such an odd railway width? Because that was the width English railroad-building expatriates brought with them to America. Why did the English build them this wide? Because the first British rail lines were built by the same people who built the

> "For I know the plans I have for you," declares the Lord, "plans to prosper you and not to harm you, plans to give you hope and a future."
>
> *Jeremiah 29:11*

pre-railroad tramways, and that's the gauge they used. Why did they use that gauge? Because the same jigs, tools, and people who built wagons built the tramways and used the standard wagon-wheel spacing. Wagon-wheel spacing was standardized due to a very practical, hard-to-change and easy-to-match reality. When Britain was ruled by Imperial Rome, Roman war chariots, in true bureaucratic fashion, all used a standard spacing between their wheels.

Over time, this spacing left deep ruts along the extensive road network that the Romans built. If British wheel spacing didn't match Roman ruts, the wheels would break. The Roman standard was derived after trial-and-error efforts of early wagon and chariot builders. They determined the best width that would accommodate two horses was four feet eight and one-half inches. Thus the U.S. standard railroad gauge is a hand-me-down based upon the original specification for an Imperial Roman war chariot.

Can you believe it? All because we didn't want to have to think about it, because we wanted to do what was easiest in the moment, we ended up with something completely different from what we would have chosen today. And that happens in many marriages time and again if we don't take deliberate actions to get out of our ruts and spice up our existence.

It's a little known fact that you can slow down time in your relationship by doing something new. So give it a try. What can the two of you do this week that will get you out of your routine?

HARMONY

A great marriage is not when the "perfect couple" comes together. It is when an imperfect couple learns to enjoy their differences.

Dave Meurer

HAVE YOU FOUND WHAT YOU'RE LOOKING FOR?

Truth, like light, blinds.

Albert Camus

There is a saying in India, "When a pickpocket meets a saint, all he sees are the pockets." Our motives shape what we see—and don't see—around us.

Consider the fabled story of the man from Colorado who moved to Texas and built a house with a large picture window from which he could view hundreds of miles of rangeland. "The only problem is," he said, "there's nothing to see." About the same time, a Texan moved to Colorado and built a house with a large picture window overlooking the Rockies. "The only problem is I can't see anything," he said. "The mountains are in the way."

People can be blind to what others see clearly. We're all prone to this problem. We all share a tendency toward denial, an emotionally comfortable strategy that protects us from the distress that recognizing the harsh truth would bring. So we resort to filtering out information, rationalizing mistakes, avoiding responsibility. Many of us will do just about anything to steer clear of the truth if it might hurt. To make the matter of getting to the truth worse, we have ways of ensuring that people around us collude with our denial. That's especially true of our spouse. At an almost unconscious level, we can work our relationship to make sure our partner avoids honest, constructive feedback, acting as though everything is fine when in fact it is not. If we are not intentional about staying clear of this tendency, we buy the illusion of harmony at the cost of the truth. And we miss the path that could take us to emotional maturity and spiritual health.

> Do you have eyes but fail to see, and ears but fail to hear?
>
> *Mark 8:18*

So what illusion might be standing in the pathway to your well-being? Or to look at it from another angle, what is God trying to show you? How is He revealing Himself to you? What are you not seeing? Of course, you can't answer that question now. It's an answer that comes only with contemplation and time—as long as we are looking for it.

HAPPILY
EVER AFTER?

The fairytale is irresponsible; it is frankly imaginary, and its purpose is to gratify wishes, as a dream doth flatter.

Susanne K. Langer

"In this world there are only two tragedies," wrote Oscar Wilde. "One is not getting what one wants, and the other is getting it." Deep down, our greatest hope is not for fame, comfort, wealth, or power. Those rewards create almost as many problems as they solve. If you reach your goal, if your dream comes true, you're bound to eventually wake up someday and ask, "Is this it?"

We will never be happy or fulfilled until we stop measuring our real-life achievements against the dream of whatever we imagined would make us happy. It's what Daniel Levinson called the "tyranny of the dream."

Each of us developed this dream when we were young. Maybe it was planted by parents or teachers, or maybe by our own imaginings. The dream was to someday be truly special. We dreamed that our work would be recognized, that our marriage would be perfect and our children exemplary. We may have dared to dream we'd be famous or affluent.

If we've been hit by a major jolt—diagnosed with cancer, for example—our dream has been deferred while we hope for a cure. But whatever we are dreaming of, we keep holding out hope that it will be realized and the fairy tale will be brought to completion. But, as Anais Nin reminded us, "We've been poisoned by fairy tales." They don't come true.

The dream can never make us happy. Even if you reach your goals to become the success you imagined, you're likely to feel empty. Why? Because our greatest hope is not for fame, comfort, wealth, or power. These are shallow hopes. Our greatest hope is far deeper. Our greatest hope is for meaning.

What does this have to do with your relationship? Everything. You've no doubt hung hopes—perhaps very high hopes—on your relationship. You've got your own version of the fairy tale you want to write together, and it's all about living happily ever after, right?

But truth be told, it will be the meaning you create together that matters most. Sure, the rewards and pleasures you experience as part of your dream are great blessings, but don't take your eyes off the meaning of your relationship in the eyes of God. That's where the ultimate dream becomes real.

> Much dreaming and many words are meaningless. Therefore fear God.
>
> *Ecclesiastes 5:7*

So where do you find your meaning? By creating harmony—especially around your purpose as a couple. In fact, what we are proposing is nothing short of building a compass for your relationship—a compass in the form of a marital mission statement.

We know this may sound intimidating, or at the very least corporate, but it's easier than you think. Simply begin with the words: "Our purpose as a married couple is . . ." We know that could lead a hundred different directions, but how would you finish that sentence stem? What comes to mind first? Take a stab at it. There are no right or wrong answers. This is simply a start in the process of articulating the mission of your marriage. So draft some ideas and don't get hung up on making this the perfect and ultimate statement. You're not writing it in stone.

Many corporations make a practice of revisiting their mission statement every so often. They study their aims and then measure their performance at regular intervals to be sure they've not fallen out of sync with their mission statement. As couples, we need to do the same thing. A purpose statement keeps us from drifting aimlessly. It keeps our marriage on track. It affords the meaning that is sure to bring the enduring joy.

ABOUT THE AUTHORS

 Drs. Les and Leslie Parrott, psychologists and marriage and family therapists, are #1 *New York Times* best-selling authors and creators of the most widely used premarriage program in the world—*Saving Your Marriage Before It Starts*—trusted by more than a million couples and translated into more than twenty languages. Their renowned SYMBIS Assessment has been called a "game changer." *Love Talk*, *Your Time-Starved Marriage*, and *Crazy Good Sex* are among their landmark best sellers. Each year they speak live to more than fifty thousand people and have been featured on *Oprah*, *CBS This Morning*, *TODAY*, CNN, *The View*, and in *USA Today* and the *New York Times*. Les and Leslie live in Seattle, Washington, with their two sons. Learn more at **LesandLeslie.com**.

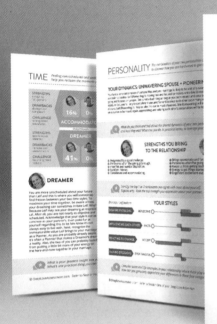

Report for:

BRIE & LEIF JENSEN
Married: 7/13/2005   Date Completed: 8/17/2016

DeepLoveAssessment.com

Take the Deep Love Assessment
for just **$35 per couple** at
Outreach.DeepLoveAssessment.co
and receive a FREE download,
"10 Secrets to Hot Monogamy."

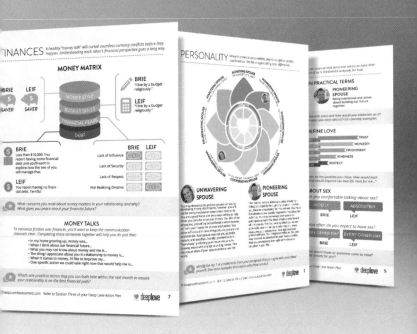

ou won't find a more personalized and powerful elationship assessment than DEEP LOVE.

ch of the four sections of the report is essential to deepening the lationship with lasting, positive results:

Personality—because it's the best way to enhance empathy

Communication—because it's the lifeblood of love

Conflict—because every couple has friction

Adaptability—because even good relationships bump into bad things